HOLIDAY GIFTS from a COUNTRY KITCHEN

by

Mary Reynolds Smith

©Potpourri Press
Greensboro, North Carolina 27404
Printed in U.S.A.

Table of Contents

Introduction

Christmas, more than any holiday, any season, is a time of traditions— holly, kissing under the mistletoe, Christmas trees and caroling, eggnog, fruitcake and, above all, the giving of gifts.

Our family has, as all families do, our own personal variations of the age-old traditions, plus a lot more— some that have been passed down through so many generations no one knows how they began; others that started at various times while I was growing up. (We'd do something one year that was a success, repeat it the next and by the third year, a new family tradition had been born.) Still others date from the first Christmas my husband and I shared.

When I was small, much of our Christmas activity centered around gifts, as I suppose it does in many families. I'm grateful, however, that the emphasis was always on the giving, not the gift. Since I was a child of the depression years, most gifts were, of necessity, those we could make ourselves. And most of the making was done in mother's kitchen.

This was natural enough because mother always cooked to share. If she was baking a pie, her recipe made two so daddy could take one to a neighbor while she finished cooking her meal. We didn't have much in those years, but mother's cooking always included extra for someone who had less than we did. Often it was as simple as a batch of hot bread sent off with some freshly churned butter and homemade jelly. Other times when pork or beef on the farm was slaughtered, the gifts were bigger— packages of fresh meat that shared our good fortune and food with many friends. But all these things, for mother, were just normal neighborly sharing. When it came to what she called "real" presents, she went to work in earnest, calling in the whole family to help.

And she made Christmas gifts all year. From cold weather to cold weather, as she canned and pickled and preserved (teaching her two daughters as she went), she talked of Christmas. She encouraged us to remember what each relative and friend liked so it could be made especially for them.

The prettiest of the red and green watermelon rind pickles, the jars with the most perfectly round tomatoes, strawberry jam with the brightest color, the thickest, spiciest catsup— all these and the best of other things were put aside, each marked for the person whom it would most please. I learned then, without being conscious really of what I was learning, that the best gift is one carefully chosen (whether bought or made) to especially suit the person to whom it is given. Then the cliche "it's the thought that counts" becomes very true indeed.

Gifts that are made with the hands and given from the heart are always appreciated and remembered with fondness. They are not, however, inexpensive. Good ingredients are costly and preparation requires time, a precious commodity for everyone. Good-food gifts are not only time-consuming to make, they are often difficult to deliver—far more trouble than the gift you buy, charge and have sent. But they say in a way that nothing else can "From me to you with love." They say "I care enough to share a part of me with you." And what could be more rewarding to both the one who gives and the one who receives?

Today I still make many of my gifts in the kitchen, and I love doing it. From a purely selfish standpoint, it offers much. There is something infinitely satisfying about working in a kitchen filled with aromas of good food gifts in the making and listening to Christmas carols on the stereo while others are out fighting crowds of tired shoppers and harrassed sales people, often to settle for spending too much for a gift they like too little. As a "bonus," my good-cook husband Clay often joins me and we spend a long weekend afternoon and evening in a warm and happy joint gift-making session. It's self-rewarding in another way, too. When I give a gift I've made, I know the happiness of having shared something of myself, which is after all, the essence of "giving."

Finally, there's another "dividend." I find myself, as I use the family recipes each year, enjoying my freshly wakened memories of mother and grandmother and aunts who made these same things long ago. My recipe file represents a potpourri of friends (old and new) as well as family, and the

5

use of friend's special recipe often causes me to interrupt my baking to place a call or write a note that's long over-due. I realize, too, that I find a deep-down satisfaction in the knowledge that young nieces and nephews and friends, with whom I've shared my recipes, will be using them and reliving happy memories many, many years from now.

So, whether you're an expert cook or someone who just "gets by" in the kitchen, I hope you'll try making some of your gifts this year. It will make your holiday season more memorable and more meaningful. And if you share your recipes with those who want them, you'll be doubly blessed.

Every December we find ourselves wishing we could hold on to the spirit of Christmas all year long. Discovering the joy of giving from your kitchen will help you do just that. For you may soon find yourself giving a "kitchen" gift at other times of the year. You'll remember birthdays you used to ignore because it was too much trouble to shop, and you'll send along a little something from your kitchen to mark special times in the lives of friends. And little by little, you may find that you are, as my mother did, "thinking Christmas" all year long.

Some of the recipes here need to be made early in the year; others can be made at any time, and quite a few are perfect for those years when a busy schedule, a family emergency, or just plain procrastination, keeps you from doing anything about Christmas until the last minute. Some recipes are old family favorites; others are quite new, but all have been carefully chosen and tested.

Regardless of which you try, I hope that— as you use the recipes— you'll capture in your kitchen some of the feelings of sharing and giving and love that were as tangible in mother's kitchen as the sweet and spicy fragrance of her cooking. For those feelings are, after all, the true spirit of Christmas.

Apple Cinnamon Cordial

After a pleasant dinner with friends not long ago, we were sipping liqueur and discussing our various personal preferences when someone mentioned having a recipe for an unusual cordial. When she said "Apple Cinnamon," I knew I had to try it. It makes an interesting change from the usual liqueurs, is especially nice during the holidays and makes an "intoxicatingly" good topping for vanilla ice cream, used alone or with some drained fruit. Bottled in a sparkling glass decanter, it makes a marvelous gift. Be sure to include some serving suggestions, especially if you include a small jar of drained fruit.

2½ cups chopped
 apples, cored but
 not peeled (firm
 green cooking
 apples are best)
3 sticks cinnamon
 (each approximately
 3" long)
2 cups sugar
2 tablespoons water
1½ cups brandy
3½ cups dry white
 wine

Core and chop apples. Combine in heavy saucepan with cinnamon, tied in a cheesecloth bag, and water. Simmer over medium heat, covered, for about 10 minutes. Add sugar and stir to dissolve. Remove from heat and cool. Pour wine and brandy into a half gallon glass container. Add the cooled apple mixture. Cover loosely; label, date and store in a cool, dry place from 2 to 4 weeks.

After the cordial has aged, strain it into one or more decorative bottles or containers for gifts. Remove cinnamon and bottle the drained fruit in small glass jars to use yourself or to include with your gift decanters. If you give the fruit, include a suggestion for using as a topping for ice cream or pound cake. It makes a fantastic quick dessert that's guaranteed to please.

Festive Fruit Punch

Makes approximately 1½ gallons (without ginger ale or soda)

This is my sister's punch recipe and is, I think, the best I've ever tasted. Even non-punch lovers like it. "As is," it's a delightful and suitable refreshment for any occasion. Should you like something stronger, its tart flavor makes it an excellent mixer for various alcoholic beverages. It freezes well so it can be made ahead (or saved if it's leftover) and, with the addition of extra ginger ale or soda, it can be stretched if your crowd grows larger or thirstier than you expected. I cannot begin to guess the number of people with whom it's been shared, nor the number of varied occasions at which it's been served. It's nice to have on hand for the holidays and a jug of it makes a great family gift since it's popular with both children and adults.

SYRUP
4 cups sugar
4 cups water

JUICES
64 ounces pineapple juice
64 ounces orange juice (preferably fresh, but canned or bottled will do)
4 7½-ounce bottles frozen lemon juice

Optional
3 pints ginger ale or club soda

To make syrup, combine sugar and water and bring to a boil. Reduce heat slightly, but continue to boil for 10 minutes. Remove from heat and cool.

Combine cooled syrup with fruit juices and mix well. Refrigerate until ready to use.

When ready to serve, add 1 pint of ginger ale or club soda* to each half gallon of punch.

*This can be eliminated or increased, according to personal taste.

If giving as a gift, be sure to include serving suggestions.

9

Liqueurs

Visiting friends in Florida some years ago, we were enjoying after-dinner drinks when I expressed envy at their being able to purchase so many different kinds (that option was not available in my home state at the time). My hostess laughed and then admitted that she had made the "kahlua" I was drinking. I was incredulous. It had never occurred to me that I could make liqueurs and I was delighted to learn how she did it. In the years since I've added to my liqueur recipes and three are included here for your holiday enjoyment. A small decanter of any one of them will make a delightful Christmas gift. Keep an eye out at yard sales and flea markets for unusual bottles and/or liqueur glasses. They'll make perfect gifts to go along with your homemade liqueur.

COFFEE LIQUEUR

Makes approximately
3 pints

4 cups sugar
2 cups water
2/3 cup instant coffee
  powder or crystals
1 fifth of vodka or
  rum*
1 vanilla bean

*Vodka will give you a drink more like the Mexican varieties, while rum will give you a "Jamaican type" liqueur. Light or dark rum may be used, depending upon your personal preference.

Stir together the sugar, water and coffee in a heavy saucepan. (Do not use aluminum.) Bring mixture to a full boil. Remove from heat, skim off the foam that has formed and cool completely. Pour into a half gallon glass container and then add the vodka or rum and vanilla bean. Label, date and store in a dark, cool place for at least 2 to 3 weeks, preferably longer. When ready to use, remove the vanilla bean and pour into glass containers which can be tightly corked or sealed.

ORANGE LIQUEUR

Makes approximately
1½ pints

3 large oranges
3 cups vodka
1½ cups superfine
    sugar

Using a sharp knife or citrus peeler, pare away the orange part of the rinds of three oranges. (Be careful to get the thin outer orange part of the rind only.) Blot rind on paper towels and put in a quart jar with 2 cups of the vodka. Fasten tightly, label and date. Store in a cool, dark place for two days, or until vodka absorbs the flavor and color of the peel. Remove the peel and add sugar. Shake to dissolve. Add remaining 1 cup of vodka, seal and store in cool, dark place for at least one month. When ready to give, transfer to decorative bottles or decanters and label.

CREME DE MENTHE

Makes approximately
½ gallon

2½ pounds sugar
1½ quarts water
1 ounce oil of
    peppermint
2 cups vodka or grain
    alcohol
few drops green food
    coloring

Combine sugar and water in a heavy saucepan and bring to a rolling boil. Reduce heat, but continue boiling mixture until it looks clear and slightly syrupy. Allow to cool completely. Stir in peppermint, vodka and food coloring and mix well. Pour into half gallon glass container, label, date and store in cool, dry place for at least a month. When ready to use, pour into decanters, seal and use for serving, cooking or for unusual presents.

11

Mulled Wine or Cider

Even if it didn't taste so good, mulled wine or cider would almost be a "must" at Christmas because, simmering on the stove, it spreads a spicy holiday aroma throughout the house. Keep a pot on your stove for unexpected drop-in guests or give a jug to a friend. It's really a lovely thing to do at Christmas.

SYRUP

1¼ cups sugar
½ cup plus 1 tablespoon water
24 whole cloves
2 3" sticks of cinnamon
1 crushed nutmeg
2 lemons (use peel only)
1 large orange (use peel only)

2 cups lemon juice, heated
2 quarts red wine or cider

To prepare the syrup, peel orange and lemons very thinly and combine peel with sugar, water and spices in a heavy saucepan. Place over medium heat and bring to a boil. Reduce heat slightly, but continue to boil for 5 minutes. Remove from heat and strain.

Place back over low heat and add 2 cups hot lemon juice and 2 quarts of wine or cider, and continue to heat (but do NOT let boil) until very hot. If serving reduce heat to very low so that the liquid will stay very hot but will not boil. If using as a gift, cool, bottle and refrigerate until ready to present it to friends with suggestions for heating and serving.

Beef and Horseradish Spread

When I was growing up, we carried our lunches to school and, looking back, I marvel at my mother's ingenuity in coming up with enough variety to keep three children happy with school lunches five days a week. This basic recipe was one of our favorite sandwich spreads. Now, it often appears at my parties in finger sandwiches or as a spread for crackers. With the addition of the beef broth, it becomes less thick and makes a spicy dip for fresh vegetables or chips.

Packed in a crock or other attractive container, this makes a great gift, especially for the person who has lots of drop-in guests during the holidays. (Be sure to include instructions for refrigeration.) And if you're feeling really generous, include a holiday tin filled with crackers (homemade ones would be sensational) or chips.

1 12-oz. can of corned beef or
1½ cups leftover corned beef, ground
½ cup mayonnaise
¼ cup horseradish, drained
3 tablespoons prepared Dijon type mustard
1 tablespoon grated onion
3 tablespoons sour cream
3 tablespoons beef broth (optional)

In a medium size mixing bowl, mash corned beef with a fork. Add all other ingredients and continue to mix until well blended. Refrigerate, covered, until ready to use. This will keep, refrigerated, for at least a week, so it can be made before the last-minute holiday rush sets in.

Remove from refrigerator and allow to soften slightly before serving.

Cheddar Potted in Port

Makes
approximately
2 cups

A small crock of this delightful wine-cheese spread is sure to please almost anyone on your gift list. Make extra because once you taste it, you'll want some to serve yourself. Recipe can be doubled.

**1 pound cheddar
    cheese shredded
¾ cup port wine
¼ pound sweet butter
¼ cup port wine**

Put shredded cheese in a bowl and pour ¾ cup port over it. Cover tightly and refrigerate overnight. The following day, drain the port from the cheese, reserving it. Cream butter and cheese together until well blended. Continuing to beat, slowly pour in the drained port and beat until the mixture is smooth and creamy.

Fill small containers. Cut rounds of parchment paper to fit tops of containers. Soak papers in ¼ cup port until well saturated. Place one round on top of each cheese-filled container. Cover tightly with lids and store in the refrigerator. This keeps well for weeks so make it well ahead of the Christmas rush.

Chili Cheese Dip

Makes
approximately
5 cups

A small container of this will delight friends who enjoy "Tex-Mex" cooking and you can govern just how "fiery" you want to make it by the amount of chili powder and pepper you add. Serve it topped with a dash of sour cream and surrounded by taco chips or give a small jar or crock of it to a friend with a huge bag of tortilla-type chips and suggestions for enjoying.

1 medium onion,
   chopped very fine
1½ tablespoons butter
   or margarine
1 can (15½ oz.) chili-
   without beans
1 pound sharp
   cheddar cheese,
   shredded
1 8-ounce package
   cream cheese,
   softened
1½ tablespoons chili
   powder
¼ teaspoon black
   pepper *or*
dash of cayenne
   pepper

Saute minced onion in butter or margarine and set aside to cool. Combine chili and softened cheeses and beat, with mixer on medium speed, until well blended. Add onions, chili powder and pepper and stir to mix. Pack into containers, cover tightly and refrigerate at least overnight before serving or giving.

Cream Cheese Balls

Makes 2 balls

An unusual cheese ball with fruit and nuts, this stores well for up to two weeks in the refrigerator. Keep one on hand for holiday guests and give one to a friend. Wrapped in clear plastic wrap and topped with a bright bow, it's a delightful gift.

1 8-ounce package of
   cream cheese,
   softened
1 6-ounce can
   crushed pineapple,
   drained very dry
1 tablespoon finely
   minced onion
½ cup finely chopped
   pecans
1 teaspoon seasoned
   salt
½ cup finely chopped
   pecans

Combine softened cream cheese with drained pineapple, onion, seasoned salt and ½ cup nuts mixing until all ingredients are well blended. Refrigerate for about 15 minutes. Form into two balls, roll in ½ cup chopped nuts and wrap in clear plastic wrap. Refrigerate until ready to use.

Spicy Spinach Dip

Makes
approximately
1¼ cups

So good that even confirmed spinach-haters will like it. And it's a pretty color to serve anytime, but especially during the holidays. Enjoy it at your own parties or give a container to a friend who entertains often.

½ cup mayonnaise
1 3-ounce package
   cream cheese,
   softened
1 tablespoon lemon
   juice
¼ teaspoon salt
¼ teaspoon finely
   minced garlic
½ teaspoon finely
   minced onion
¼ teaspoon Italian
   herb seasoning
¼ teaspoon paprika
2 cups (lightly packed)
   cut up spinach

With your blender at medium speed, blend mayonnaise, cream cheese, lemon juice and spices until smooth. Add spinach, about ½ cup at a time and process on high until mixture is smooth.

This is also very easy to do in the food processor. Simply put all ingredients in bowl, fitted with metal blade and process until mixture is smooth.

Cover and refrigerate until ready to use.

Pimento Pickle Cheese Dip

This is another of my party dips that grew out of a sandwich spread my mother used in our school-day lunches. Of course, her pimento cheese was homemade and I usually use the delicatessen's, but the result is still good. The flavor of this colorful dip compliments all fresh vegetables but is, I think, especially good with cauliflower and celery.

It's a terrific last-minute gift, packed in a glass jar or a reusable covered bowl and labeled with refrigeration and serving suggestions. For a really special gift, center your bowl on a tray or platter, surround it with fresh vegetables for dipping, cover the whole thing securely with clear plastic wrap, top with a holiday bow and hand-deliver. The recipient is sure to love it— for unexpected company or just for family nibbling to offset the ever-present holiday sweets.

1½ cups pimento
   cheese
¾ cup sour cream
½ cup salad pickles,
   drained
1 teaspoon
   Worcestershire sauce
2 teaspoons prepared
   Dijon type mustard
dash of hot pepper
   sauce (optional)
salt and pepper to
   taste (optional)

Remove pimento cheese from refrigerator and allow to soften slightly. Mix it together with the next four ingredients, using a wooden spoon or fork, until well blended. Add pepper sauce, salt and pepper if desired. I personally prefer the dip without them, but I leave that to your particular taste. Refrigerate, covered, until ready to use.

Cheese Wafers

Makes
approximately
3 dozen

Because of early failures with them, I avoided trying to make cheese wafers up until a few years ago when I tasted these. The sister-in-law of a friend brought a huge container of them to an impromptu "let's everybody bring something and get together" summer party, and when I asked her how she found time to make them, she gave me her recipe. Since then, it's become one of my tried-and-true stand-bys. They're easy and fast to make, practically "no-fail," relatively economical and universally popular. What more can you ask?

Also, they keep well (up to two weeks in a tightly covered container) and freeze beautifully, so you can make a good supply well ahead of the holiday rush. Tins of these make wonderful gifts for the people who are not especially fond of sweets. In fact, almost anyone will welcome them as a nice taste-change from the many cookies and candies in the house at Christmas.

½ cup butter or margarine, softened
1 cup all-purpose flour, measured before sifting
1 cup shredded sharp cheddar cheese, softened
½ teaspoon salt
dash of cayenne pepper *or*
a few drops of hot pepper sauce (optional)
1 cup unsweetened rice cereal bits
paprika (optional)

Preheat oven to 325°.

Combine softened butter, cheese, flour, salt and pepper (if used), mixing with a wooden spoon or by hand until all ingredients are well blended. Work in cereal bits. Chill dough for about 15 minutes.

When ready to bake, form dough into small balls and place about 1½" apart on ungreased cookie sheet. Flatten each ball with a fork, pressing first one way and then the other to make a criss-cross pattern. (You may need to dip the fork in flour occasionally.) If using white cheddar, you may wish to dust the tops with paprika for added color. Bake 12-15 minutes until *very* lightly browned. Allow to cool thoroughly on a wire rack before storing in tightly covered container. When packing in container, it is a good idea to separate layers with wax paper.

19

Salted Coconut Strips

A perfect gift for the person who loves crisp, crunchy— and unusual— taste treats... and a pleasing addition to your own holiday snacks. They keep for up to two weeks in a tightly covered container stored in a cool, dry place. Be sure to keep plenty for yourself (you'll be surprised at how hard it is to stop eating them) and package those you wish to give in gay holiday tins or in tightly sealed plastic bags tied with bright Christmas ribbons.

1 medium large
    coconut (about 1
    pound weight)
salt

To prepare your fresh coconut, pierce two or three holes in the "eye" indentions in one end of the coconut by using an ice pick or by tapping a small nail with a hammer. Place over a container and let the milk drain out. Refrigerate this to enjoy later as a drink or to use in other holiday baking. Put the coconut in a preheated 325° oven for 10-15 minutes. Remove; wrap in a heavy cloth and tap with a hammer. The coconut will break easily and the outer husk will fall away. For use in this recipe, try to keep the coconut in as large pieces as possible. With a sharp knife or vegetable peeler, remove the thin brown skin. Rinse the coconut meat and dry.

Preheat oven to 275° Again using a very sharp knife or vegetable peeler, shave off the thinnest possible strips of coconut.

Place strips in a layer in a shallow baking pan (a 15" x 10" x 1" jelly roll pan works well), sprinkle with salt and bake approximately 45 minutes or until

strips are dry, curled and golden brown. Take out of the oven and salt again. Allow to cool completely before storing in a tightly covered container. You will need to repeat this process with the remaining strips to avoid layering them too thickly in the pan. If you wish to bake both pans at one time, put a pan on each rack of your oven and turn and reverse the pans about twice during the 45 minute baking period.

NOTE: Baked without salt, the strips make a pretty and a good garnish for holiday cakes and pies. You may want to do a few separately for this purpose.

Parmesan Rosettes

A few years ago after eating far too many crisp, sugary rosettes at a friend's 25th wedding anniversary celebration, I bought a rosette iron and became "hooked" on the delightful cookies I could make with it. However, I had to experiment and since I like "cheesy" things, I came up with this version of the ever-popular treat. With the many shapes available now for the iron, you can make wonderful holiday goodies (trees, bells, etc.) that are pretty, as well as delicious, additions to any "happy hour" buffet table. And a bright Christmas tin of them makes a lovely gift for anyone, but especially for the person who doesn't eat sweets. You can make them a week or ten days before using because they keep well stored in a tightly covered container.

3 eggs
1½ cups milk
1¼ cups all-purpose flour
¼ cup wheat germ
2 tablespoons grated parmesan cheese
2 tablespoons minced dried onion
1 tablespoon sugar
cooking oil for frying
1 cup grated parmesan cheese

Heat cooking oil to 375°.

Beat eggs with a rotary beater or wire whisk. Beat in milk. Add flour, wheat germ, 2 tablespoons cheese, onion and sugar, beating until thoroughly mixed.

In a heavy saucepan, deep skillet or deep fryer, heat oil to 375° Heat iron in oil, shake off excess oil and dip hot iron in batter, coming up to within about ¼" of top of iron (do not let batter come over top of iron). Put iron back in oil for 30-60 seconds or until rosette is golden brown. Lift iron out of oil, tipping slightly to allow excess fat to drain off. With fork, push rosette gently off iron onto paper towel lined rack. Sprinkle with parmesan cheese and allow to cool completely on wire rack. Reheat iron and continue making rosettes. If batter becomes too thick, add a small amount of milk. When rosettes are completely cool, store in tightly covered container.

Bacon Bites

These are fun to serve or give because most people have trouble guessing what they are or how you've made them. If you like bacon—and most everyone does— you'll love these crunchy tidbits. They're great with any cold drink and you really will find it difficult to "eat just one." Stored in a tightly covered tin, they'll stay crisp and delicious for up to a week, so keep some on hand for instant snacks or delightfully different gifts.

**12 strips of bacon,
each cut in half
24 square saltine
crackers**

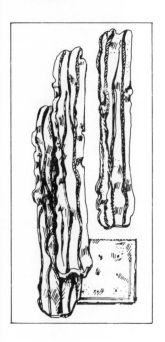

Preheat oven to 400°.

Wrap each cracker with a half-strip of bacon and place on broiler pan or a wire rack set over a shallow pan to catch drips (I use a wire cooling rack set over an old jelly roll pan).

Bake 12-15 minutes, turning once so that both sides brown. When golden brown, remove from oven and serve hot or allow to cool completely on paper-towel covered wire rack before storing in tightly covered container. These can be returned to a 400° oven briefly for warming before serving or served cold. They're good either way.

Sesame Crisps

Makes
30 4"-5"
crackers

If you like crackers as well as I do, you can make a meal (albeit a some-what fattening one) with just those nutty tasting crisp rounds, sweet butter and hot tea. They're perfect for luncheons, dinners or just for munching. They're easy to make, though a bit time-consuming, and they can be stored in a tightly covered container for a week to ten days without loss of flavor.

When I was small, mother made these, not with sesame seed, but with coarse salt sprinkled on top and we loved them. A good many years later when a blood pressure problem made salt a "no-no" for me, I altered her recipe, eliminating the salt and adding sesame seed and now they're once again my favorite cracker.

A bright tin filled with these makes a marvelous gift for the person on your list who just doesn't care for sweets. And if that person is extra-special, you might add a small container of herbed or whipped sweet butter.

1¾ cups all-purpose flour
½ cup cornmeal
2 tablespoons sugar
½ teaspoon soda
¼ teaspoon salt
¼ cup butter or margarine
½ cup water
2 tablespoons vinegar
¼ cup butter or margarine, melted
½ cup sesame seed

Preheat oven to 375°.

Put flour, cornmeal, sugar, soda and salt into a mixing bowl and, with a pastry blender, cut in ¼ cup butter or margarine until mixture looks like very coarse meal. Mix together water and vinegar and stir into flour mixture. Knead with hands until well blended. Dough will be very soft.

To make with a food processor, put first five ingredients into processor bowl. Add butter cut in small pieces. Using steel blade, turn processor on and off until mixture resembles coarse meal. With the motor running, add water/vinegar mixture. Turn off at once and transfer dough to floured surface, work-ing in a little additional flour if dough is too soft to handle.

With hands, divide dough into small balls. On floured surface, using a rolling pin, roll each ball into a 4"-5" very thin round. (Do not worry if edges are slightly uneven.) Transfer each cracker (using a wide spatula) to ungreased or foil lined baking sheet, placing them about 1" apart. Brush each round with melted butter and sprinkle with sesame seed. Using the spatula, press sesame seed firmly into crackers. Bake 10 minutes or until lightly browned. Allow to cool completely on wire rack before storing in tightly covered container.

Spicy Walnuts

I have a friend who turns up her nose at the sugary-cinnamony nuts I love so much, but adores these spicy ones. If you have a non-sweet eater on your list, a jar of these will make a perfect gift.

⅜ cup vegetable oil
2 teaspoons chili
    powder
¾ teaspoon ground
    cumin
½ teaspoon tumeric
dash of cayenne
    pepper (optional)
3 cups walnuts
salt (optional)

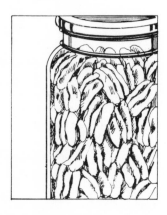

Preheat oven to 275°

In a heavy deep skillet, combine all ingredients except nuts and salt, and place over medium heat. When oil is hot (do not let burn), add nuts and stir until well coated. With a slotted spoon, transfer nuts to a shallow ungreased baking pan and place on top rack of oven. Bake for 10-15 minutes until nuts are crisp. If using salt, sprinkle on hot nuts and place on wire rack. Allow to cool completely before storing in a tightly covered container. These keep well, in a cool dry place, for up to a month, so you can do them early.

Wheat Crackers

Makes
6-8 dozen

You may wonder why anyone bothers to make homemade crackers when the grocery shelves are filled with every imaginable shape and flavor. For one thing, homemade ones are infinitely better. For another, you know exactly what you put in yours which is comforting in these days when even confirmed label-readers often have difficulty identifying the ingredients in a canned or boxed product. Finally, they are fun and easy to make and a box of them with a crock of your special cheese spread or a small cheese ball makes an outstanding holiday gift.

1 cup whole wheat
  flour
1 cup all-purpose
  flour
¼ cup plus 1
  tablespoon sugar
2 teaspoons baking
  powder
1 teaspoon baking
  soda
½ teaspoon cream of
  tartar
½ teaspoon salt
½ cup butter or
  margarine
¾ cup buttermilk

Preheat oven to 350°.

If mixing by hand, combine dry ingredients in a large bowl and, using a pastry blender or two knives, cut in the butter or margarine until the mixture is coarse crumbs. Add buttermilk and stir with fork. Turn dough out onto lightly floured surface and roll and cut as directed below.

If using a food processor, put all dry ingredients together with butter or margarine in processor bowl fitted with steel blade. Turn the processor on and off quickly until mixture resembles coarse meal. With motor running, pour buttermilk through the feed tube, turning the motor off as soon as the dough whirls itself into a ball. Place on floured surface.

Roll dough as thin as possible and cut with a biscuit cutter or, if you want something "fancier," use cookie cutters of your choice. Using a spatula, transfer crackers to an ungreased baking sheet, placing about 1" apart. Prick each cracker several times with a fork and bake 12-15 minutes or until very lightly browned. Allow to cool completely on a wire rack and store in tightly covered container.

27

Brown and Serve Rolls

Makes
24 rolls

In many ways, my mother was a very old fashioned lady, but in others she was a woman ahead of her time. She loved her job as a buyer in our town's book store and it's the one thing she insisted on doing in the face of my father's displeasure. She was the best "scratch" cook I've ever known, but she was always the first to try one of the "new-fangled" mixes when they began to come on the market or to try a time-saving short cut in an old family recipe. So it's not strange that mother was baking "brown and serve" rolls before you could buy them. It was simply her way of continuing to serve the yeast rolls we loved when she didn't have time to make them. A plastic bag of these from your freezer is sure to be a welcome gift for a friend during the busy holiday season. And you'll love having them on hand for your own family when the last-minute rush gets you down.

1 package active dry yeast

¾ cup warm water (110° to 115°)

¾ cup milk, scalded and cooled to lukewarm

⅛ cup plus 1 tablespoon sugar

2 teaspoons salt

¼ cup shortening, melted

2½ cups sifted all-purpose flour

2 cups (approximately) sifted all-purpose flour

Sprinkle yeast on warm water and stir to dissolve. Add milk, sugar, salt, shortening and 2½ cups flour, stirring to mix. Beat until smooth. Stir in enough of the remaining 2 cups of flour to make a soft dough that leaves the sides of the bowl as it is mixed.

Turn dough out onto floured surface and knead until it is smooth (about 5 minutes). Place in greased bowl, turning dough to coat all sides. Cover and put in a warm place to rise until doubled in bulk (about 1½ hours).

Shape rolls as you prefer* and place about 2½"-3" apart on a greased baking sheet or in greased muffin tins. Cover and let rise again until doubled in size (45 minutes to an hour).

Shortly before ready to bake, preheat oven to 275°. When rolls have doubled in size, bake for 20-25 minutes. (Do not brown.) Cool on wire rack.

Wrap as many rolls as desired in one package, wrapping securely in plastic wrap or foil and freeze. These will remain frozen for up to 3 months without loss of flavor and can be refrigerated for several days. When ready to use, preheat oven to 400° Brush tops of rolls with melted butter or margarine and bake for 8 to 10 minutes until golden brown.

*Rolls can be shaped in a number of ways. Several are:

1. Simply shape dough into round 2" balls.
2. Shape dough for each roll into three small balls and place in greased muffin tin for Cloverleaf rolls.
3. Shape dough in 2" balls. Roll between floured hands to about 4" long and roll ends to taper. Curve slightly and place on baking sheet.

29

Christmas Raisin Buns

Makes
12 large
buns

This recipe is a favorite of mine because it's the very first yeast bread I ever baked—more years ago than I care to remember. And once I had made these successfully, it became a family tradition to enjoy them with milk or coffee while we opened our first presents on Christmas morning.

½ cup milk
½ cup sugar
½ teaspoon salt
¼ cup butter or
    margarine
2 envelopes active
    dry yeast
½ cup very warm
    water (120°)
1 teaspoon sugar
2 eggs beaten
5 cups all purpose
    flour
1 teaspoon nutmeg
1 cup seedless golden
    raisins
¼ cup butter or
    margarine, melted

Combine milk, sugar, salt and butter or margarine in a heavy saucepan and cook, over medium heat, until butter and sugar are dissolved. Cool to lukewarm (110°). Put ½ cup warm water (120°) into large bowl. Sprinkle yeast and 1 teaspoon sugar over it; stir until yeast dissolves. Let stand about 10 minutes or until mixture bubbles. Stir in cooled mixture and beaten eggs.

Beat in 2 cups of the flour and the nutmeg until smooth. Stir in raisins; then beat in remaining 3 cups of flour to make a stiff dough. Turn onto floured board and knead until smooth and elastic, adding a little extra flour if necessary to keep dough from being sticky.

Place in lightly greased bowl, turning to coat all sides of dough. Cover with a cloth and let rise in a warm, draft-free place until doubled in bulk (about 1 hour). Punch down and turn onto floured board. Divide into 12 pieces and shape each into a ball. Place on ungreased baking sheet and let rise until doubled in size.

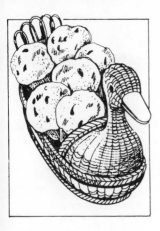

Preheat oven to 350°, and bake 15 minutes or until buns sound hollow when tapped. Remove and brush tops with melted butter or margarine.

If making for later use, allow buns to cool completely at this point, wrap in foil or plastic wrap, label, date and freeze. When ready to serve, preheat oven to 350° and heat rolls for 10 minutes.

If using as a gift, be sure to include thawing/warming instructions.

Cardamom Twist

Makes
3 loaves

Should you ever have occasion to call Potpourri Press, the company that published this book, your call will in all probability be answered by a lady who is as charming as she sounds. In addition to being a whiz on the phone, Yvonne is an accomplished baker and often shares her creations with the office staff. Everyone's favorite is her Cardamon Twist which really has to be tasted to be believed. Absolutely nothing could make a better Christmas gift than a loaf of this, wrapped in clear plastic and tied with a bow.

2 packages active
  dry yeast
2 tablespoons sugar
2 cups very warm
  (120°) water
1 egg
½ cup less 2
  tablespoons sugar
2 teaspoons salt
½ cup butter or
  margarine
½ teaspoon
  cardamom seeds,
  crushed fine
6½ cups all-purpose
  flour
1 tablespoon milk
1 egg
sesame seed or poppy
  seed (optional)

Mix yeast, water and 2 tablespoons sugar and let stand for five minutes. Using a heavy-duty mixer, blend 1 egg, sugar, salt and margarine or butter until smooth. Add cardamom. Mix in one half the flour, adding it alternately with yeast mixture. Continue adding the flour until you have used it all. If your mixer is not a heavy one, you may need to stir in the last of the flour by hand.

Turn out onto floured board and knead for one minute. Place in a greased bowl, turning it to coat all sides, cover and let stand in a warm, draft-free place for approximately 1 hour, or until doubled in bulk.

Punch down and turn out onto floured board. Let rest for five minutes. Divide dough into 9 equal parts. Roll each part between your hands to make a 12" rope. For each loaf, braid three pieces together and tuck ends under. Place on

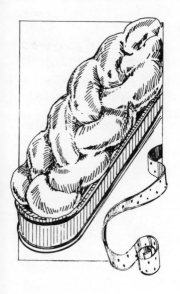

greased baking pans, cover with a cloth, place in a warm place and let rise until doubled again (approximately 45 minutes).

Preheat oven to 350°. Beat 1 egg with 1 tablespoon of milk and, using a pastry brush, spread on the top of each loaf. Sprinkle with sesame seed or poppy seed as desired. Bake until golden brown (approximately 25-30 minutes).

With a spatula, transfer bread to wire rack and allow to cool completely. Store in plastic bag.

This freezes well for up to three months, sealed in plastic bags.

Make-Ahead Biscuits

Makes
20-2½"
biscuits

While I much prefer yeast bread to biscuits, I am married to a man who likes biscuits so well that he, like a good friend of ours, claims never to have eaten a really bad biscuit. And although he'll settle for canned ones, he much prefers the homemade variety, which takes more time. My compromise is this recipe which lets me make quantities of homemade biscuits at one time and freeze them for quick use. They're nice to share anytime, but especially at Christmas when a bag of them from your freezer is sure to delight a friend who is extra-busy.

4 cups all-purpose
  flour
2 tablespoons baking
  powder
1½ teaspoons salt
2½ teaspoons sugar
½ teaspoon baking
  soda
1 16-ounce container
  sour cream
½ cup shortening

Mix flour, baking powder, salt, sugar and baking soda together in large bowl. With pastry blender or two knives, used scissors fashion, cut in sour cream and shortening until mixture resembles coarse meal. With hands, knead dough to mix thoroughly (you may need to add a little water— a teaspoonful at a time— if dough is too dry). Roll, on a floured surface, about ½" thick and cut biscuits with a floured cutter.

IF BAKING AT ONCE:
Preheat oven to 425°. Place biscuits about 1 inch apart on ungreased baking sheet and bake 10-15 minutes until lightly browned.

IF FREEZING FOR LATER USE:
Place biscuits on baking sheet, cover with clear plastic wrap and freeze. When biscuits are frozen, remove from sheet and place as many as desired in a plastic bag, seal tightly and keep frozen.

When ready to use, preheat oven to 425°, place biscuits on ungreased baking sheet and bake for 20-25 minutes until lightly browned.

If using biscuits as a gift, include instructions for keeping them frozen and for baking.

34

Crème Fraîche

On my birthday recently, I found a totally charming gift on my desk left there by a much younger-than-I friend and co-worker. When I peeked into the blue plaid cloth in the pretty handled basket, I found marvelous croissants, a jar of a famous-name strawberry jam and— best of all— a jar of creme fraiche. It evoked images of leisurely Sunday morning repasts for me to enjoy with absolutely no effort. And I loved it. Later, when I told her how much I enjoyed it, she gave me her ultra-simple method of making the Crème Fraîche which differed from the traditional way I knew. I include both of them here. Whichever you use, a jar of creme fraiche will make a lovely gift for almost anyone, especially if you accompany it with other "goodies" and package it as attractively as my friend Barb did.

BARB'S CREME FRAICHE (Version I)

1 cup heavy cream
1 cup commercial
    sour cream

Combine the two ingredients, shaking to mix thoroughly and let stand at room temperature overnight or until thickened. Stir again and refrigerate until ready to use.

CREME FRAICHE (Version II)

2 cups heavy cream
2 teaspoons
    buttermilk

Combine the ingredients, shaking to mix thoroughly. Let stand at room temperature for a day (or longer if necessary) until it thickens. Cover and refrigerate until ready to use. It will keep for 2 to 3 weeks in the refrigerator.

Ice Cream Sauces

My husband Clay loves ice cream. Unfortunately, he doesn't enjoy having the same flavor more than a few nights in a row, so I try to keep a variety in my freezer. Sometimes, however, that isn't possible either because of lack of space, failure to get to the store, or my own absent-mindedness. The solution? I always have vanilla and try to keep a variety of sauces to top it with. I'm including three of my favorites here. They're easy to make, keep for a long time, and one— or all— would make a great gift for any ice cream lover.

For an extra-special present, try tucking a small jar of sauce in the top of an inexpensive glass sundae dish, wrapping in cellophane and topping with a bow. Or package jars of sauces with a set of small bowls in ice cream colors... or tie an ice cream scoop around the top of a jar of sauce with a gay Christmas ribbon. Use your imagination and have fun.

FUDGE SAUCE

Makes approximately
   5 cups

2 cups unsweetened
   cocoa powder
1½ cups granulated
   sugar
1 cup brown sugar
2 cups heavy cream
1 cup butter
   (margarine may be
   substituted, but real
   butter gives more
   flavor)
2 teaspoons vanilla

Combine cocoa and sugars in a heavy saucepan. Add butter, cut into small pieces, and cream. Place pan over medium heat and bring to a boil. Allow to boil for 90 seconds, stirring constantly. Remove from heat. Cool slightly and stir in vanilla. Allow to cool for another few minutes. Pour into small decorative glass containers with tight fitting lids, label and store in the refrigerator for holiday giving. Keeps well for 2-3 weeks in the refrigerator.

HONEY GINGER SAUCE

Makes 3½-4 cups

2 cups honey
½ cup water
¾ cup chopped
    candied ginger
1 cup pecans,
    coarsely chopped

Stir honey and water together in a heavy saucepan and bring to a boil over medium heat. Stir in ginger and pecans and simmer for 1 minute. Pour into hot sterilized jars and seal with regular canning lids. This can be stored on the shelf— doesn't need refrigeration and keeps for a long, long time.

ORANGE-NUT SAUCE

Makes approximately
    6 cups

1 cup light corn syrup
1 tablespoon grated
    orange rind
1 cup orange juice
2 cups honey
1 cup pecans,
    coarsely chopped
½ cup blanched
    slivered almonds
1 cup walnuts,
    coarsely chopped

In a heavy saucepan, stir together syrup, orange rind, orange juice and honey. Bring to a boil and remove from heat. Stir in nuts until completely mixed. Spoon into glass jars or other containers that can be covered tightly and refrigerate until ready to serve or give.

Peaches in Bourbon

Several years ago I ordered a small "keg" of peaches preserved in bourbon from a well known Texas store to add to my husband's Christmas "goodies." He loved them, but rebelled at ordering more for himself, so we set about trying to duplicate them. We had a lot of fun and ate a lot of peaches while we were coming up with this recipe, but I think you'll like it. The peaches make a great instant dessert, topped with whipped cream and served with thinly sliced pound cake or crisp cookies. And the liquid in which they're canned makes a marvelous topping for vanilla ice cream. With gift jars, be sure to include some serving suggestions. And if they're going to someone who likes to cook, include a copy of the recipe.

6 pounds peaches
water
1 tablespoon ascorbic
acid crystals
1 orange
6 cups sugar
3 cups bourbon

Blanch peaches about 2 pounds at a time in boiling water for 30 seconds. Place in ice water to chill. Peel, halve and pit fruit. Combine 1 gallon of water with ascorbic acid, and soak fruit in the solution.

In the meantime, using a sharp knife or citrus parer, peel the orange part of the rind away in thin strip. Cut into 7 pieces and reserve.

Mix 6 cups of water and 6 cups of sugar in a large heavy saucepan and bring to a boil over medium heat. Add fruit, about 8 pieces at a time and reduce heat. Simmer 5 minutes. Pack fruit in hot, sterilized jars, filling to within ½" of top. Repeat with remaining peaches and put one strip of prepared orange peel in each jar.

Boil remaining syrup in pan till a candy thermometer registers 220°. Cool for 5 minutes. Measure 3 cups of the syrup into a medium saucepan. Add bourbon and stir to mix. Place over medium heat and bring just to simmering point. Pour hot syrup over peaches in jar, leaving ½" head room. Seal and process in hot water bath for 10 minutes. These are best if you let them age for several weeks before opening and serving.

Pear-Pineapple Marmalade

Makes 10
half pint
jars

There may be something better with hot bread and butter than home-made marmalade, but I don't know what it is. This particular combination of flavors is, I think, especially good. It's simple to make and a jar is sure to please almost anyone on your gift list.

5 pounds pears
  (slightly under-ripe
  ones)
1 medium pineapple
2½ teaspoons grated
  lemon rind
3 tablespoons lemon
  juice
1/3 pound
  crystallized ginger,
  chopped very fine
5 cups sugar

Peel and core pears and cut into slices. Peel and core pineapple and chop coarsely. Combine fruits, lemon rind and juice, ginger and sugar in a heavy saucepan. Over medium heat, bring to a boil, stirring constantly. Reduce heat and cook uncovered until mixture thickens (about 1½ hours), stirring occasionally to prevent sticking.

Spoon into hot sterilized half pint jars, seal and process in a hot water bath 15 minutes. Label and date when cool and store in a cool, dry place... ready for holiday giving.

Clay's Chili

Makes
14-16 pints

My husband's chili has always been popular with our friends, but I'd never thought of using it for gifts until several years ago. When I suggested it, Clay didn't think much of the idea, but the reaction of friends who received jars of chili at Christmas convinced him. You may want to cook chili for an informal Christmas crowd. Or you may cook it ahead to can or freeze for gifts. Whatever you do, I hope you enjoy it as much as we do.

½ cup bacon drippings
   or cooking oil
5 pounds onions,
   chopped finely
1½ pounds green peppers,
   chopped finely
8 pounds ground beef
   (ground twice)
1 pound sausage
5 1-pound cans
   tomatoes, mashed
3 6-ounce cans
   tomato paste
   dissolved in
1 quart water
½ cup prepared mustard
1 quart beef broth
¼ cup Burgundy wine
¼ cup lemon juice
1 tablespoon hot sauce
2 tablespoons salt
1 tablespoon black
   pepper
3 tablespoons dried basil
3 tablespoons oregano
2 tablespoons finely
   minced garlic
2 ounces ground cumin
2½ ounces chili powder

Heat the drippings or oil in a large heavy soup pot. Add chopped onions and peppers and cook over low heat until they appear transparent. Add beef and sausage, stirring and continuing to cook until all meat is browned. With a large spoon, remove as much excess fat as possible. Add all the rest of the ingredients **except** chili powder and simmer for about 2 hours, stirring as necessary. Stir in chili powder and simmer for about 1 more hour, continuing to stir as necessary to prevent burning.

Ladle into containers, label and freeze. Or fill hot, sterilized jar and process in a pressure canner at 15 pounds for 30 minutes. Allow jars to cool, label and store in a cool place. For gifts, we prefer to give the chili "as is" without beans so that it can be used in the recipient's favorite way. If you're serving it at once as chili con carne, add 3 1-pound cans kidney beans and simmer for another 15-20 minutes before serving.

41

Spicy Catsup

Everyone sings the praises of my friend Ruby's homemade catsup and when you try it, I know you'll see why. It captures all the goodness of summer sun ripened tomatoes in a spicy condiment to add joy to winter meals. Ruby suggests it as a topping for meat loaf, among other things. However you use it, you'll love it. And a jar of this rich red catsup will delight anyone on your Christmas list.

4 quarts peeled
   tomatoes
1 large sweet green
   pepper
½ cup chopped
   onions
1 cup granulated
   sugar
1 cup brown sugar
1/6 cup salt
1¼ pints vinegar
1½ teaspoons
   cinnamon
1 teaspoon allspice
1 teaspoon ginger
1 teaspoon nutmeg

Combine all ingredients in a large heavy pot and bring to a boil. Reduce heat and simmer, stirring very often, for 3½ hours.

Ladle into hot sterilized jars and process in a hot water bath for 5 minutes. Cool, label and store until ready to enjoy or to give away for others to enjoy.

Flavored Mustards

Flavored mustards are available in the specialty foods section of many stores, but the ones you make at home are less expensive and in many ways better. They make a delicious condiment served with cold meats, turn a sandwich into a gourmet treat and serve as a quick, simple but delightful glaze for meats. One of these is a tangy sweet/sour spread; the other, a spicy French style mustard. A jar of one or both will be a sure-to-please gift.

WINE MUSTARD

Makes 2 half pint jars

¾ cup sugar
¾ cup dry mustard
½ cup vinegar
½ cup dry white wine
3 eggs

Using a wire whisk, combine all ingredients in the top of a double broiler over simmering water or in a small heavy saucepan, whisking until very smooth. Cook until mixture is smooth and thick (about 8-10 minutes). Spoon into hot, sterilized small jars and cover tightly. Refrigerate until ready to use.

ONION MUSTARD

Makes 3 half pint jars

2 cups finely chopped
    onions
2 cloves garlic,
    minced
2 cups dry white wine
4 ounces dry mustard
2 tablespoons honey
2 tablespoons
    vegetable oil
1 teaspoon salt
¼ teaspoon pepper

Combine onion, garlic and wine in a heavy saucepan and bring to a boil. Reduce heat and simmer for 15 minutes. Remove from heat and cool for 15 minutes. Pour into blender and process until mixture is smooth. Pour into a bowl and set aside. In the meantime, combine mustard, honey and oil in the saucepan, whisking until smooth. Stir in the onion/garlic mixture, salt and pepper, whisking until well blended. Bring to a boil, stirring constantly. Continuing to stir, reduce heat and cook until mixture thickens (about 5 minutes). Spoon into hot, sterilized jars, seal and process in a hot water bath for 7 minutes. Cool, label and store.

43

Watermelon Relish

Makes 7-8
half-pint
jars

When my brother, sister and I were small, mother always had a plentiful supply of watermelon rind to make her sparkling jars of red and green pickles. As we grew older and less anxious to cut every melon that came out of the patch, there was less and less rind available. And even though we raised the melons, mother simply could not bear to throw away the inside in order to make pickles from the outside. Finally my sister suggested we try making a relish from the "meat" of the watermelon and after a good many hot afternoons in the kitchen and a lot of melons, this recipe was born. With much the taste of watermelon rind pickles, the texture of a relish, and a pretty red color, it soon became— and has stayed— a holiday favorite. Good with almost any meat, a small jar will make a delightful and unusual gift.

1 large watermelon
   (approximately 20
   pounds)
3¾ cups sugar
2 cups vinegar
2 limes, sliced thinly
½ cup lime or lemon
   juice
1 teaspoon ground
   cloves
1 teaspoon ground
   cinnamon

With a large spoon, scoop melon out in chunks or slice the melon, cut away the rind and cut melon into chunks. Working with about 1 cup of melon at a time, put the chunks in a square of cheesecloth (use a double thickness) and squeeze out the liquid. Remove seeds and put the pulp into a large heavy saucepan. You should have approximately 14 cups.

If you wish to use a food processor (which I find much easier and quicker), remove seed from melon when you are cutting it into chunks. Use the steel blade and process about 2 cups of melon at a time, cutting the processor on and off until the melon is in small lumpy pieces. Do **not** over-process or you will end up with a puree. Pour contents of processor through a double layer of cheesecloth, squeezing to remove all liquid. Transfer pulp to a heavy saucepan.

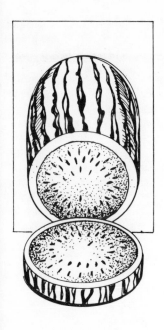

Add sugar and vinegar and bring to a boil. Reduce heat and simmer for approximately 30 minutes, stirring as needed.

In the meantime, slice limes very thinly, cover with a small amount of water, bring to a boil. Drain and repeat the process two more times. This will keep limes from tasting bitter. Drain limes and add to melon mixture, together with lime juice, cinnamon and cloves. Continue to cook for approximately 30 minutes longer until relish is thick. Stir often.

Spoon relish into hot, sterilized half pint jars, filling to within ¼" of top. Seal and process in a hot water bath for 20 minutes. Be sure to label and date before storing in a cool place.

Sweet-Hot Tomato Relish

My husband loves good food and, bless his heart, does not hesitate to brag on what he likes. If someone else has prepared it, he's often quick to suggest that I get the recipe to use in my own kitchen, and I've found that most people are very generous with their recipes, even treasured old family "secrets." Such was the case some years ago when our old and dear friend Frances gave him a jar of her freshly canned Sweet-Hot Tomato Relish when he stopped by for an afternoon visit. Clay sampled it that evening at dinner and was so enthusiastic in his praise that I asked for the recipe. Frances, saying it was "nothing," she'd been "making it for years," gladly shared it with me and now that I too have made it for years, I share it with you.

1 gallon tomatoes
½ cup hot peppers
½ gallon sweet green
   peppers
1 pound of onions
½ cup vinegar
½ cup granulated
   sugar
1 cup firmly packed
   brown sugar

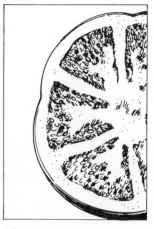

Peel tomatoes. (Plunge washed tomatoes into boiling water for a few seconds, remove and rinse under cold water. Skins will slip off easily.) Put tomatoes in a heavy saucepan with a very small amount of water, cover and cook until done. Set aside. Meanwhile, remove seeds from peppers (it's best to use gloves when handling hot peppers to avoid skin irritation) and put them through a food grinder or process, using steel blade, in food processor. Process onions through food grinder or in food processor. (You should have approximately 2 cups ground onions.)

Combine peppers and onions in a large bowl and sprinkle with salt (using several teaspoonsful). Cover with hot water and soak for 20-30 minutes. Drain in a colander and rinse with cold water.

Combine tomatoes, peppers, onion, vinegar and sugars in a large heavy pan and over medium heat, bring to a boil. Reduce heat and allow to barely simmer, covered, for 3 to 4 hours until relish is thick. Stir occasionally to avoid sticking and burning. Spoon into hot sterilized jars, seal and process in a hot water bath for 15 minutes for half pints, 20 minutes for pints. When cool, label and store.

This recipe can be easily doubled if you wish to make the relish in large quantities.

Pepper Jelly

Makes six
half pints

Unsalted crackers spread with whipped cream cheese and topped with hot pepper jelly is both a pretty and delicious addition to any hors d'oeurve table. And while you can buy pepper jelly, the homemade is much, much better— and less expensive. Because of the clear red and green color, it's especially pretty for holiday gifts.

1 cup seeded green
   peppers, ground
¼ cup hot peppers
   (with a few seeds
   left in), ground
6½ cups granulated
   sugar
1½ cups vinegar
1 bottle Certo
food coloring— red or
   green

Clean the green peppers and chop finely or grind. Clean the red peppers, leaving a few seeds in and chop or grind. (It's a good idea to wear gloves when working with hot peppers to guard against skin irritation.) Mix peppers with sugar and vinegar in a heavy saucepan and bring to a boil. Reduce heat slightly and boil for five minutes. Remove from heat and cool 15-20 minutes. Strain and bring back to a boil. Boil, stirring constantly, for two minutes. Remove from heat; add the certo and red or green coloring as desired. Pour into hot sterilized jars and seal.

Meanwhile, melt 1 block of parafin wax in top of a double boiler. Pour a thin layer of wax over the top of jelly in each jar, tilting the jar so that parafin touches the edge all the way around in order to seal the jar thoroughly. Store in a cool, dry place.

Hot Chow Chow

My sister, as far as food tastes were concerned, would have been perfectly happy living in the middle of Mexico. Nothing was too pepper-hot for her. This was true of my brother-in-law Howard also and when the two of them got together at family affairs, we refused to let them come near the food with a pepper shaker or pepper pod in hand. One day another brother in law, Harvey, brought each of them a small jar of chow chow which a friend had made and which he insisted was sufficiently hot to please them. It did and for years, gifts of Harvey's friend's Chow Chow were a family tradition. The friend was finally kind enough to share the recipe which I continue to make each year for our friends who are addicted to hot, peppery foods.

1 quart finely
  chopped cabbage
1 quart finely
  chopped hot
  peppers
1 pint finely
  chopped onions
2 cups granulated
  sugar
4 tablespoons salt
4 tablespoons
  mustard seed
2 teaspoons celery
  seed
1 quart vinegar

Combine chopped cabbage, seeded and chopped peppers, peeled and chopped onions with all other ingredients in a large bowl. Stir together to mix well, cover and let stand overnight. Spoon into hot, sterilized half pint jars, seal and process in a hot water bath for 10 minutes. Cool, label and store in a cool, dry place.

49

All-Fruit, No-Bake Fruitcake

Makes
15-16
cups*

This recipe is so old, I don't know it's origin. I'm not at all sure my mother knew where it came from. She made it because her mother had made it. It was just one of those things we always had at Christmas, and we called it fruitcake. I have friends that insist it's candy. Whatever the name, it's a delicious, nutritious "confection" that can be eaten as soon as it's made, but which grows better with age. And it keeps, carefully wrapped and stored in a cool dry place, practically forever so that you can make it even before Thanksgiving while you're still waiting for the grocery stores to start displaying the candied fruits for your traditional baked fruitcakes.

It can be formed in small loaves, large loaves or tiny individual balls. Loaves can be wrapped in clear wrap and tied with a bright bow; balls can be packed in tins or other attractive containers. You can give a little or a lot. Whatever you do, it will be a welcome and an unusual gift.

CAKE

12 ounces dried apples
12 ounces pitted prunes
12 ounces dried apricots
12 ounces dried peaches
12 ounces dried figs
1 large or 2 small oranges, seeded but with rind
16 ounces pecans
16 ounces English walnuts
½ cup sugar

Put fruit and nuts through a food grinder and in a large bowl mix all ingredients together thoroughly. (The easiest way to do this is with your hands. In fact, it's the only way to get it thoroughly mixed in my opinion.) If processing fruits and nuts in a food processor, add about 1 tablespoon from the sugar to each batch.

If you are making loaves, line pans with two strips of foil, one going each way and leaving ends protruding so they can be used to lift cakes out of pans later. Pack filling into pans to desired height. Cover and weight (canned goods from your pantry shelf will do nicely) overnight. Remove weights; remove from pans and wrap securely with foil or plastic wrap. Store in cool dry dark place for 4 to 6 weeks. To serve, slice thinly with very sharp knife.

50

COATING
1/4 cup granulated
   sugar
1 teaspoon prepared
   grated orange peel

OR
1/8 cup granulated
   sugar
1/8 cup finely ground
   pecans
1 teaspoon prepared
   orange peel

If making balls, pinch off small pieces of the mixture and roll between your palms to form a small round ball. Then roll the balls in one of the coating mixtures before storing.

Note: The quantity given will coat approximately 75-80 small balls.

Mix ingredients together and place in shallow plate. Roll fruitcake balls in mixture and place in storage container.

*You can divide this quantity up in a variety of ways, depending upon your personal preference. You can pack 6-8 cups (depending upon depth) in a 9"x 5" loaf pan. A 3"x 5" miniature loaf pan (my preference) holds about 1½ cups packed full. And 1 cup of the mixture will make approximately 24-30 small balls.

Japanese Fruitcake

My great aunt Mary moved to Atlanta, Georgia as a young bride and lived there for her long and happy married life. Along the way, she acquired a southern accent thick enough to cut with a knife and collected a group of recipes for marvelous southern "goodies." I eagerly awaited her annual holiday visit since she was my favorite aunt, but mother was sometimes less than enthusiastic because Aunt Mary did tend to take over her kitchen. Once she discovered that my father (her favorite nephew-in-law), who did not like traditional fruitcake, loved her Japanese Fruitcake, it became a tradition and she either made it (or supervised the making of it) on every visit. Make it shortly before you plan to serve it or give it because it really shouldn't be kept longer than 2-3 days.

CAKE

3¼ cups all-purpose flour

½ teaspoon salt

1 teaspoon baking powder

1 cup butter or margarine

1 teaspoon vanilla

2 cups sugar

4 large or 5 medium eggs

1 cup milk

1 cup light raisins

1 teaspoon cinnamon

1 teaspoon allspice

½ teaspoon cloves

¾ cup freshly grated coconut

Preheat oven to 350°

Line bottoms of 8" round cake pans with two layers of wax paper or parchment and set aside. Sift flour, salt and baking powder together and set aside. With electric mixer, cream butter thoroughly. Add vanilla and add sugar very slowly, continuing to beat until well blended. Add eggs one at a time, beating after each addition. Add flour and milk alternately, mixing well. Put 1½ cups batter into each of two of the prepared pans and bake 25 minutes or until a cake tester comes out clean. Place on wire rack to cool. In the meantime, add raisins and spices to remaining batter and mix thoroughly. Again, put 1½ cups of batter into each of prepared pans. (You may remove layers from first two pans and prepare them for these two layers.) Bake last two layers for 25 minutes or until tester comes out clean, and cool on wire rack.

While layers are cooling completely, prepare the filling as follows. Using a citrus parer or vegetable peeler remove

52

FILLING

2 cups sugar
Peel of 2 lemons
1 cup water
¼ cup lemon juice
2 tablespoons
  cornstarch
4 cups freshly grated
  coconut*
1 20-oz. can crushed
  pineapple, drained

a thin layer of peel from lemons. Add this to the sugar in a heavy saucepan, stir in water and bring to a boil over medium heat. Reduce heat and allow to simmer for 5 minutes. Remove from heat and discard the lemon peel. In a measuring cup, mix together the cornstarch and lemon juice and stir this into the sugar mixture. Bring back to a boil and cook for 1 minute, stirring almost constantly. Remove from heat and cool. Stir in coconut and pineapple.

To assemble the cake, put one plain layer on plate and spread with ¼ of the filling. Place a spice layer on top of this and again spread with ¼ of the filling. Repeat with plain layer and second spice layer, spreading ¼ of the filling on each layer. Sprinkle ¾ cup coconut on top of the filling on the top layer, patting it in with your hands. Cover and refrigerate until ready to serve. If using as a gift, be sure to include instructions for refrigerating the cake until it is served.

*Preparing a fresh coconut is not my favorite occupation, but the result is good enough to make the labor worthwhile. For me this is the easiest way to do it. With an ice pick or with a small nail and hammer, pierce two or three holes in the "eye" indentions in one end of the coconut. Place over a container and let milk drain. Refrigerate this to enjoy drinking later or to use in other baking. Place the coconut in a preheated 325° oven for 15 minutes. Remove; wrap in a heavy cloth and tap with a hammer. The coconut will break easily and the husk will fall away. With a sharp knife, pare the brown skin and hand grate the meat or process it in the blender or food processor.

Red Velvet Cake

My husband's niece Pat, who decorates gorgeous cakes that taste as good as they look, made the first Red Velvet Cake I ever saw. I loved it then and I still do. Not only is it good, it's such a pretty cake for Christmas. It's fun to serve because almost everyone likes chocolate and, wrapped in clear plastic wrap and topped with a bright bow, it makes a wonderful "family" present for good friends or neighbors to enjoy through the holidays.

CAKE

1 cup butter or
    margarine
1 teaspoon vanilla
1½ cups sugar
3 large eggs
2 ounces red food
    coloring
3 tablespoons
    unsweetened cocoa
    powder
1 teaspoon salt
2½ cups cake flour,
    sifted
1 cup buttermilk
1 teaspoon baking
    soda
1 tablespoon vinegar
1 making Frosting
    recipe
candy canes or
    peppermints
    crushed for garnish
    if desired

Preheat oven to 350?

Grease and flour three 8" pans and set aside. Using electric mixer, beat butter until creamy. Add vanilla and sugar slowly, continuing to beat until well mixed. Add eggs, one at a time, beating thoroughly after each addition. With mixer on low speed, slowly add food coloring. Add cocoa and salt, mixing well. Add flour alternately with milk. In a measuring cup, mix the baking soda and vinegar and add to batter, beating well. Divide batter evenly between the three pans and bake 25-30 minutes or until a cake tester comes out clean. Partially cool on wire rack before removing from pans. Allow layers to cool completely before frosting.

FROSTING

2 cups milk
½ cup plus 1
   tablespoon all-
   purpose flour
¼ cup milk
1 cup butter or
   margarine
1 cup vegetable
   shortening
2 cups sugar
4 teaspoons vanilla

To make the frosting, heat 1¾ cup of the milk until it barely bubbles. Remove from heat. Put the flour in another sauce-pan and stir in the ¼ cup milk with a wire whisk until mixture is smooth. Pour in the hot milk slowly, stirring constantly, and bring mixture to a boil over medium heat. Remove from heat and allow to cool, stirring occasionally. In the meantime, using electric mixer, beat butter until creamy. Continuing to beat, add sugar and vanilla. Add the cooled milk mixture, beating thoroughly.

To assemble cake, spread about ¼ of the frosting between each layer and use the remaining frosting for the top and sides of the cake. Top of the cake can be sprinkled with crushed candy canes or peppermints if you wish.

Hawaiian Dessert Loaf

Makes two
9"x5" loaves

One of the nicest things about traveling is the chance to get to know new people, to learn about their lifestyle and to sample their food. And among the best souvenirs my husband and I have of our trips are recipes that, each time they are used, wake fresh memories of good times shared. This particular "goodie" came home with us from our one and only Hawaiian trip and each time I bake it, the combination of flavors evokes memories of happy days and nights in that magic place.

This is a dense, moist, very rich "bread-cake," so you can bake it in small loaves for really lovely gifts. Refrigerated, it keeps for up to a month and it freezes beautifully, so you can make it well ahead of the holiday rush. With a gift loaf, be sure to include a note saying that it needs to be refrigerated and a suggestion to slice it thinly.

5 jars (3¼ oz. size)
  macadamia nuts,
  chopped
2 cans (15½ oz. size)
  crushed pineapple,
  well drained
1½ cups sweetened
  flaked coconut
1 cup plus
  2 tablespoons flour
1 cup plus
  2 tablespoons sugar
1 teaspoon baking
  powder
¾ teaspoon salt
  (eliminate if salted
  nuts are used)
5 eggs
1½ teaspoons vanilla

Preheat oven to 350°.

Grease loaf pans and cover bottom with wax paper or greased heavy brown paper cut to fit.

Mix chopped nuts, pineapple and coconut in a large bowl. Sift flour, salt and baking powder over mixture. Add sugar and mix gently to coat all nuts and fruit. In a separate small bowl, beat eggs until foamy. Stir in vanilla and pour over mixture in large bowl. Stir with a wooden spoon until thoroughly mixed. Spoon into pans and bake approximately 1 hour.

Turn loaves out on wire rack to cool. Wrap in plastic wrap or aluminum foil and store in refrigerator or freezer.

This mixture can be baked in miniature loaf pans for very attractive gifts or in cupcake pans (especially the small ones). The small "tarts" can then be · packed in tins for gift-giving.

56

Surprise Cupcakes

Every so often, I "rediscover" cupcakes— usually when I need to bake a birthday cake and am short on time and energy or when I'm recruited at the last minute to provide refreshments for an impromptu gathering. Cupcakes just seem so much easier to me than a cake. And when they're a hit, as they always are, I wonder why I don't bake them more often. Cupcakes are a marvelous compromise between a big cake and a small cookie. These are among my favorites and because they're delicious without frosting, are ideal for a gift that must be packaged for mailing.

FILLING

8 ounces cream
   cheese, softened
1 egg
1/2 cup granulated sugar
1/2 cup chocolate chips
   and
1/2 cup pecans,
   chopped
or
1 cup pecans, chopped
or
1 cup chocolate chips

BATTER

1 1/2 cups all-purpose
   flour
1 teaspoon soda
1/4 teaspoon salt
1 cup sugar
1/4 cup unsweetened
   cocoa
1 cup water
1/2 cup oil
1 tablespoon vinegar
1 1/4 teaspoons vanilla

TOPPING

1/4 cup pecans finely
   chopped

Preheat oven to 350°

To prepare the filling, beat together cream cheese, egg and sugar until smooth and creamy. Stir in chocolate chips and/or nuts. Set aside.

To prepare the batter, sift flour, soda, salt, sugar and cocoa together in mixing bowl. Add water, oil, vinegar and vanilla and beat until thoroughly mixed. Line muffin cups with paper baking cups and fill each cup approximately one-third full with chocolate batter. Put a spoonful of filling on top of each.

Sprinkle finely chopped nuts on top and bake approximately 35 minutes or until a cake tester inserted in center of cupcake comes out clean. Allow to cool completely on rack before placing in covered container.

Tropical Delight

This is a good moist cake that keeps well, refrigerated for several days, so you can make it more or less at your convenience during the busy holiday season. It's good enough for dessert for a "company" meal, easy enough to make for drop-in guests, and pretty enough to use as a gift.

BATTER

3 cups all purpose flour

2 cups sugar

1/2 teaspoon salt

1 teaspoon baking soda

1 1/4 teaspoon cinnamon

3 eggs, beaten

1 1/2 cups salad oil

2 teaspoons vanilla

1 8-ounce can crushed pineapple, with juice

1 cup chopped pecans

2 cups chopped bananas

FILLING/FROSTING

1 8-ounce package cream cheese, softened

1/2 cup butter or margarine

1 1/2 teaspoons vanilla

1 pound confectioner's sugar

1/2 cup pecans, finely chopped for top of cake

Preheat oven to 350°.

To prepare batter, grease and flour three 9-inch pans and set aside.

Combine flour, sugar, salt, soda and cinnamon in a large bowl. Stir in beaten eggs and salad oil (do not beat), stirring until dry ingredients are moist. Stir in remaining ingredients, mixing well. Divide batter evenly between three pans and bake 25 to 30 minutes or until a cake tester comes out clean. Cool on rack for 10-12 minutes before removing from pans. Allow to cool completely before filling and frosting.

To prepare filling/frosting, beat together cream cheese, butter and vanilla until smooth and creamy. Add confectioner's sugar and beat until light and fluffy. Use approximately one-half of the mixture between the layers of the cake and the other half to frost the cake. Sprinkle chopped nuts on top of cake.

Joann's Persimmon Pudding

Fills a
1½-cup
mold

The man who is the moving force behind Potpourri Press, the company that published this book is, among other things, quite a gourmet as well as a gourmet cook. He is also married to a lady who is gorgeous to look at, wears clothes better than a model, is an accomplished musician and is also a gourmet cook (Doesn't sound fair, does it?). When the contents of this book were being discussed, he asked about the recipe for Persimmon Pudding and then said Joann (his wife) makes the best one I've ever tasted. With a recommendation like that, I couldn't resist asking her if she would share and she very generously did. So here's Joann's Persimmon Pudding... I think you'll agree it lives up to it's billing.

1 cup persimmon
   pulp
1 cup sugar
2 tablespoons melted
   butter
1 egg, beaten
juice of ½ lemon
1 teaspoon vanilla
¼ teaspoon cinnamon
½ teaspoon salt
1 cup sifted flour
2 teaspoons baking
   soda
½ cup milk

Blend all ingredients together in order given above until thoroughly mixed. Pour into a greased 1½ cup mold, cover and steam for 2 hours.

This is delicious served warm or it may be wrapped securely in foil and frozen. When ready to serve, remove from freezer and steam for 1 hour.

P.S. While enjoying a sumptuous lunch with George and Ellie Shearing, the subject got around to "Persimmon Pudding." I had the "galley proofs" of this marvelous book at home with me, so I grabbed it to see if "Joann's" recipe had made it. Sure enough, there it was, but the truth is, Joann had only made it once (absolutely divine!), as it is Ellie Shearing's recipe that she so generously had shared with us. Caught red handed! But she did say it was O.K. to use it, provided I send her a few books. Done!

David Grimes
Potpourri Press

Frozen Strawberry Mould

My husband's sister Carrie is, undoubtedly, one of the best cooks I know. Fortunately she is as generous in sharing her recipes and kitchen secrets as she is in everything else, so many of my best desserts were made first in her kitchen. This is just one of many. I include it here for several reasons. It's pretty; it can be made ahead and tucked in the freezer until you're ready to use it; and it has a nice fresh light taste which contrasts delightfully with most of the heavier holiday desserts. Serve it at a Christmas meal or transfer it from your freezer to a friend's for an unexpected gift. Either way, it's sure to be a success.

CRUST

½ cup butter or
    margarine
1 cup flour
¼ cup brown sugar
½ cup chopped
    pecans

FILLING

1 10-ounce package
    frozen strawberries
2 egg whites
1 cup sugar
2 teaspoons lemon
    juice
1 cup cream, whipped
or
1 8-ounce carton of
    frozen whipped
    topping

Preheat oven to 350°.

To prepare crust, soften butter and blend in all ingredients until well mixed. Put into 8" square pan and bake 20 minutes, stirring occasionally. Mixture will be crumbly. Remove and set aside to cool.

To prepare the filling, blend together in a large bowl the strawberries, egg whites, sugar and lemon juice. Then beat, with mixer in high, for 10 to 12 minutes. (You will have a lot of volume.) Fold in whipped cream or softened frozen whipped topping.

Press cooled crumb mixture into a springform pan to make the bottom crust, reserving about 2 tablespoons. Spoon in filling and sprinkle remaining crumbs on top. Freeze until ready to serve. When ready to use, dip pan in hot water for several seconds and invert on plate to unmould. Holding the serv-

ing platter you wish to use carefully on top of the unmoulded dessert, invert once again, leaving the mould right side up and ready to serve or to cover with clear plastic wrap for transporting to a friend's house. If you're using this as a gift, you may want to make it in a new springform pan and, rather than unmoulding the dessert, give both it and the pan as a sure-to-please present.

Praline Crackers

Being basically a bit lazy, I love a recipe for something that is quick, easy and good. Apparently everyone else does too, for certain recipes that fit that description reappear every few years as "new" to make the rounds of young cooks all over again. Such a recipe is this one. I'm always surprised that anything so easy can be so crispy and good. Do try these. They're fun to have on hand for the holidays and a tin of them will make a terrific last-minute gift.

24 whole graham crackers
1 cup butter or margarine
1 cup brown sugar, packed
1 cup chopped pecans

Preheat oven to 350°

Arrange graham crackers in a layer in an ungreased 15"x 10"x 1" baking pan. Combine butter and sugar in a small heavy saucepan and, over medium heat, bring to a boil. Boil for two minutes. Remove from heat and stir in pecans. Spread evenly over graham crackers and bake for 10 minutes. The topping will at first look "bubbly" and then appear to "set." Do *not* overcook. Place on rack to cool, cutting crackers in half with a sharp knife while cookies are still warm. Store in a tightly covered container. These keep well for up to two weeks which is another advantage during the busy holiday season.

Raisin-Nut Squares

Bar cookies are among my favorites because they can be cut small to add to collections of cookies or larger to make quick desserts. They're good and they're easy to make. And they have the added advantages of keeping well, freezing beautifully and packing well if you're preparing a gift box that must be mailed. What more could you ask??

CRUST
½ cup butter
1 cup all purpose
    flour, unsifted
1/3 cup granulated
    sugar

FILLING
2 eggs, beaten
1 cup brown sugar
2 tablespoons all
    purpose flour
½ teaspoon baking
    powder
1 teaspoon vanilla
¾ cup raisins
3 tablespoons
    Galliano Liquore
    (optional)
¾ cup pecans,
    chopped

Preheat oven to 350°.

For crust, blend butter, flour and sugar together until smooth. Press evenly into the bottom of ungreased 8" square pan and bake for 15-18 minutes. Remove from oven.

While crust is baking, prepare filling. If using Galliano, pour over raisins and set aside. Combine eggs, sugar, flour, baking powder and vanilla, mixing until smooth. Stir in raisins and nuts. Pour over crust and return to oven. Bake 30-35 minutes until filling "sets" and browns slightly. Allow to cool completely on rack before cutting into squares. Store in tightly covered container in cool place.

Honey Almond Curls

Makes approximately 7 dozen

A mouth-watering combination of honey and almonds and apricots and all sorts of good things, these confections need to mellow for at least two weeks and improve with even further aging. That means you can make them as early as Thanksgiving, pack them away and be all ready to package them in gift containers when gift-giving time arrives. Although the list of ingredients looks long, the cookies go together easily, and the recipe makes a large quantity so you'll have plenty to keep and give away.

DOUGH
1 cup honey
2/3 cup sugar
2 tablespoons water
1 teaspoon grated
   lemon peel
2 tablespoons brandy
4 cups all-purpose
   flour, unsifted
2 teaspoons baking
   soda
1/2 teaspoon cinnamon
1/4 teaspoon cloves
1/4 teaspoon ginger
1/4 teaspoon coriander

To prepare the dough, combine honey and sugar with 2 tablespoons water in a small saucepan. Stir with a wooden spoon over medium heat until sugar dissolves. Do not boil. Allow to cool to lukewarm and stir in the lemon peel and brandy. In the meantime, sift flour with soda and spices into a mixing bowl. Add honey mixture and mix. The dough will be stiff. Knead it with your hands until smooth; form it into a ball; cover and refrigerate overnight.

Prepare the filling the following day by combining all ingredients and mixing well.

Preheat oven to 350° Working with half of the dough at one time (leaving the other half refrigerated), roll the dough into a rectangle approximately 10″ wide and 12″ long. Cut into four strips, each about 10″x 3″. Put filling in

FILLING

3 cups blanched
  almonds, ground
  finely
1 cup sugar
½ cup apricot
  preserves
1/3 cup honey
1 tablespoon grated
  lemon peel
2½ tablespoons
  lemon juice
2 teaspoons almond
  flavoring

GLAZE

1½ cups granulated
  sugar
½ cup water
½ cup confectioner's
  sugar

a mound down the center of each strip (it will take about 5 teaspoonsful for each strip). Bring the edges of the dough together over the filling and press with your fingers to seal. Turn seam side down. Cut strips into 1" long pieces with a sharp knife that you have dipped in water. Place about 1½" apart on lightly greased baking sheet. Bake 20 minutes.

To prepare glaze, combine granulated sugar and water in a heavy saucepan over medium heat. Bring to a boil, stirring as necessary. Allow to boil, without stirring until a candy thermometer registers 230° Remove from heat. Stir in confectioner's sugar and brush on warm cookies.

Store cookies in tightly covered container for at least two weeks before using.

Sesame Fingers

Makes
approximately
100

At the end of World War II, many rural communities across the United States acquired their first bit of international flavor when "Johnny came marching home" and brought with him a wife born in England, France, Italy or Germany. Our community was no exception, and I was enchanted by these girls, little older than my sister, who had been born in another land, spoke another language, and had traveled so far through countries I had only read about. And I was fascinated by the strange (to me) food they served and often brought to church and neighborhood covered dish meals. Since even at that age I was "hooked" on cooking, I asked for recipes and found that the girls, often homesick, were happy to share their family cooking secrets.

The following recipe came from one of our community's young Italian wives. A delightful biscuit/cookie, it's delicious with coffee, but perhaps even better with wine. My friend said that she, like her family, often "dunked" these in red wine before eating, but I didn't try that until I was older, thanks to my mother's intervention.

A tin of these will please almost anyone on your Christmas list and if the recipient is extra special, you may want to add a ribbon-tied bottle of wine for a super-festive gift.

4 cups all-purpose
   flour
4 teaspoons baking
   powder
½ teaspoon salt
1 cup sugar
1 teaspoon vanilla
1 cup butter or
   margarine
3 eggs
milk
2 cups sesame seed

Preheat oven to 350°.

Sift together flour, baking powder and salt and set aside. Cream butter and add sugar and vanilla, beating thoroughly. Add eggs, one at a time, beating well after each addition. With mixer on low, add flour, mixing only until it is completely incorporated and the batter is smooth. Chill for at least 30 minutes.

When ready to form cookies, pour about 1" of milk into a small bowl. Spread sesame seeds in a flat shallow pan or plate. Divide dough into fourths, working with one part while leaving the other refrigerated. Break off enough dough to make a ball approximately the size of a golf ball. On a floured surface, shape dough into a rope about 10" long and ½" in diameter. Cut into pieces 2" long and drop into milk. Remove carefully and roll in sesame seeds until pieces are completely coated. Place on foil lined baking sheet about 1" apart and bake 20-25 minutes until lightly browned. Cool on rack and store in tightly covered container for up to 1 week.

Butter Crunch Squares

These are almost sinfully good cookies that have the added advantages of being easy to make in fairly large quantities and keeping well. The buttery crunchy topping sets them apart from many other bar cookies and a tin of them will say a delicious "happy holiday" to your favorite "cookie monster" in a very special way.

PASTRY

1 cup butter or
   margarine
6 tablespoons sugar
5 hard boiled eggs
   (use yolks only)
1 teaspoon vanilla
2 cups all-purpose
   flour, sifted
½ teaspoon salt

TOPPING

1 cup sugar
1 teaspoon lemon
   juice
¼ cup heavy cream
½ cup butter (better
   if you do not
   substitute
   margarine)
1½ cups sliced
   almonds, blanched
   and toasted
1 teaspoon vanilla

Bake at 350°

Hard cook the eggs; allow to cool; peel and remove the yolks (hopefully you like hard cooked egg whites and can eat them). Put yolks through a sieve and set aside. In a large mixing bowl, cream butter and sugar together thoroughly. Stir in sieved egg yolks, vanilla, flour and salt. Press dough into a lightly greased 11"x 16" jelly roll pan and chill for 30 minutes. Preheat oven to 350° and bake 40-45 minutes (pastry will not be completely done). Remove from oven.

While pastry is cooking, prepare topping as follows. Mix sugar and lemon juice together in a heavy saucepan over low heat. Cook, stirring almost constantly until sugar is dissolved and a golden brown color (do not burn). Add cream and sugar and bring to a boil. Do not be alarmed when the sugar appears to harden; it will melt and blend with the cream and butter. Stir mixture until smooth. Stir in nuts and

remove from heat. Cool slightly and stir in vanilla. Spread topping over pastry and place pan on top rack of oven. Bake 10-15 minutes, or until topping is bubbling. Cool slightly on wire rack. With a sharp greased knife, cut into small squares (approximately 1"). Allow to cool completely before removing from pan and storing in tightly covered container. These keep well for up to two weeks stored in a cool dry place and freeze well if you wish to keep them longer.

Oatmeal Sandwich Cookies

These are definitely not the pretty little cookies usually associated with a Christmas collection. They are instead hearty he-man treats, but they are undeniably good and that seems reason enough to include them here. Another is that, for me, they are a personal triumph. I hate to think of the quantities of molasses, oatmeal and spices I used before I turned out a cookie that would stay soft without being as chewy as a caramel or completely collapsing into a pile of crumbs. Put together with a creamy filling, these make a delicious sandwich cookie, but if you're rushed, they're good "as is." If you like crispier cookies, try the variation listed. They're good, too. A box of either will delight any cookie lover on your list.

COOKIES

2/3 cup vegetable shortening

1 cup all-purpose flour

2 teaspoons baking powder

2 teaspoons baking soda

1/2 teaspoon salt

1 teaspoon cinnamon

1/2 teaspoon cloves

1/2 teaspoon nutmeg

1/2 cup sugar

2 1/2 cups quick rolled oats

1 egg, beaten

1/2 cup molasses

4 tablespoons sour cream

Preheat oven to 350°.

To make the cookies, melt shortening over low heat and set aside to cool. In a large bowl, sift together flour, baking powder, baking soda, salt, spices and sugar. Stir in the rolled oats. In a small separate bowl, beat the egg, using a rotary beater or wire whisk. Add shortening, molasses and sour cream, beating until thoroughly mixed. Pour over dry ingredients and stir with a wooden spoon until well mixed. Chill for 15-30 minutes. Drop by teaspoonful onto lightly greased or foil lined baking sheets about 2" apart. Bake 10-12 minutes. Cookies will spread and be soft and slightly puffy. Place baking sheet on wire rack to cool, or slide foil lining off onto wire rack for cooling and use pan for next batch of cookies. When cookies have cooled for several minutes, loosen with thin spatula and allow to cool completely before handling.

FILLING

⅜ cup milk
¼ cup butter or
    margarine
¼ cup vegetable
    shortening
½ cup sugar
1 egg white, unbeaten
1 teaspoon vanilla

When cookies have cooled completely, put two together, flat sides together with frosting made as follows:

Bring milk to a boil over medium heat. Remove from heat and set aside. With electric mixer, beat together butter or margarine and shortening. Add sugar and continue to beat until light in color. Add egg white and vanilla and beat thoroughly. With mixer on high, add milk slowly, beating for 3 to 5 minutes until mixture is light, fluffy and of spreading consistency.

VARIATION:
CRISP OATMEAL COOKIES

To make a crisp cookie, simply eliminate the egg when mixing the dough. The result will be a crunchy cookie that will do any cookie jar proud. Great with milk as a snack!

71

Brandy Wreaths

A deceptively simple but good little cookie that, because of its shape, is especially pretty on a holiday tray of goodies.

1 cup butter or
   margarine, softened
½ cup sugar
2½ cups all-purpose
   flour, sifted
2 tablespoons brandy

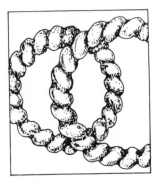

Preheat oven to 350°

Combine all ingredients, working together with your hands to make a soft dough. For each cookie, pinch off two small pieces of dough. Form each into a 5" "rope" about the diameter of a pencil. Twist the two pieces together and shape into a wreath, pinching the ends together. Repeat until all dough is used. Transfer cookies to a lightly greased baking sheet and bake 12-15 minutes until very lightly browned.

Creme de Menthe Bars

The flavors of mint and chocolate really compliment one another and this simple-to-make little cookie/candy makes good use of the combination. I have yet to find someone who doesn't like these and the green creme de menthe makes them especially pretty for your holiday table or gift-giving.

BOTTOM LAYER
½ cup butter or
   margarine
½ cup unsweetened
   cocoa powder
½ cup confectioner's
   sugar
1 egg, beaten
1 teaspoon vanilla
2 cups graham
   cracker crumbs

MIDDLE LAYER
½ cup butter or
   margarine
1/3 cup green creme
   de menthe
3 cups confectioner's
   sugar

TOP LAYER
¼ cup butter or
   margarine
1½ cups semisweet
   chocolate bits

To make bottom layer, combine butter or margarine and cocoa powder in a saucepan over medium heat. Heat, stirring until well blended. Remove from heat and stir in confectioner's sugar, egg and vanilla and mix thoroughly. Stir in graham cracker crumbs and press mixture into an ungreased baking pan or dish, 9"x 13"x 2".

To make middle layer, melt ½ cup butter or margarine and pour into small mixing bowl. Add creme de menthe and, using mixer on low speed, beat in 3 cups of confectioner's sugar, mixing until smooth. Spread over bottom layer, cover with plastic wrap and chill for at least 1 hour.

To make top layer, combine ¼ cup butter or margarine and chocolate bits in top of double boiler. Cook, stirring as needed until melted and smooth. Spread over middle layer and return pan to refrigerator. Chill for at least 2 hours or longer.

Cut in small squares and store in refrigerator. Wrap each square in clear plastic wrap, or put each square in a decorative paper candy cup and arrange in layers in a gift tin.

Toffee Crunch Fudge

A candy so super easy that it seems almost "cheat-y" to call it homemade. A very few minutes will give you a box of candy that's creamy and crunchy at the same time and sure to please almost everyone. Better make extra though because once you sample it, you won't want to give it all away.

1 pound white
  chocolate
3 oz. Toffee crunch*
1¾ cups unsweetened
  rice cereal bits

Break or cut chocolate into small chunks and melt in top of a double boiler over hot (not boiling) water, stirring occasionally with a wooden spoon until chocolate is completely melted and smooth. Remove from heat. Stir in toffee and rice cereal bits.

Spread into an 8"x 8" pan and put in refrigerator to harden. When fudge is hard, remove and let stand at room temperature for a few minutes. Score into 1" squares and cut with a sharp knife. Some pieces may break into irregular shapes, but this only seems to give the candy some of the charm of almond bark and certainly does nothing to detract from the taste.

*Available at confectioner's supply stores.

Caramel Corn

Caramel corn seems to please "children of all ages." And, actually, it's kind of fun to make. This version, my favorite, combines popcorn with nuts to make it a little extra-special. You can make enormous quantities quickly — and at the last-minute if you've put off all our Christmas cooking until the big day is right at hand. Packed in a pretty reusable container, it becomes a lovely gift... but even packaged in a plastic bag and tied with a bright Christmas ribbon, it's a much appreciated gift.

4 cups popped corn
½ cup blanched
    almonds
½ cup pecan halves
½ cup butter or
    margarine
¼ cup light corn
    syrup
2/3 cup sugar

Combine popped corn and nuts and spread on ungreased baking sheet. In a small heavy saucepan, melt butter or margarine. Stir in syrup and sugar. Bring to a boil, stirring constantly, over medium heat. Continue boiling, stirring occasionally for 10-15 minutes or until mixture turns a light caramel color. Remove from heat and stir in vanilla. Pour over corn and nuts and mix until pieces are all coated. Spread out to dry. When thoroughly cool and dry, break into pieces and store in tightly covered container.

Sugar-and-Spice Nuts

Some years ago a young girl who worked for me gave me, at Christmas, two small antique canning jars filled with delicious spicy nuts. When I expressed surprise at her cooking ability, she laughed and told me the nuts were the only thing she knew how to make. She seemed delighted to have done something I didn't know how to do and gladly shared her recipes. One is a delicious blend of nuts, sugar and cinnamon; the other— nuts, spices and orange. Both are totally addictive and make delightful gifts. They will keep for several weeks in a tightly covered container stored in a cool dry place, so make them early for holiday giving.

SUGAR AND CINNAMON PECANS

Makes 4-4½ cups nuts

4 cups pecan halves
½ cup butter or margarine
3 egg whites
½ teaspoon salt
¾ cup sugar
1½ teaspoon cinnamon

Preheat oven to 250°

Spread nuts on shallow baking pan and bake for 25 minutes. Remove from oven and pour nuts into a bowl. Put butter on hot baking sheet, tilting it to be sure it's evenly coated. Pour nuts back into buttered pan, using a wooden spoon to spread them evenly over the pan. Set aside while preparing the coating. Turn oven up to 300°

Beat egg whites until foamy. Add salt, sugar and cinnamon slowly, continuing to beat until stiff peaks are formed when you lift the mixer. Pour sugar mixture over the nuts, using a wooden spoon to spread it evenly. Put back in oven and bake 35 to 40 minutes, watching carefully. Stir nuts as necessary to keep them separated and bake until they are "dry" looking and slightly brown. Be careful and do not let them burn. Allow to cool completely before packing in containers.

ORANGE AND SPICE WALNUTS

Makes 2 cups

1½ cups
   confectioner's sugar
2 tablespoons
   cornstarch
1 teaspoon cinnamon
½ teaspoon cloves
½ teaspoon allspice
¼ teaspoon salt
1 tablespoon grated
   orange rind
1 large egg white
1 tablespoon orange
   juice
2 cups walnuts

Preheat oven to 250°

Sift first six ingredients into a mixing bowl. Stir in orange rind. In a separate bowl, beat egg whites and orange juice together until foamy. Add walnuts, stiring to coat nuts well. With a slotted spoon, remove walnuts and place on paper toweling to drain. Transfer to sugar mixture a few at a time, and roll nuts in sugar until completely coated. Place on ungreased jelly roll pans (try to keep nuts from touching) and bake for 1 hour or until dry. Place on wire rack to cool completely before storing in tightly covered container. These keep well for 3 to 4 weeks, so you can make them well ahead of the holiday rush.

Crystallized Apple Slices

Makes
3 to 4 dozen
pieces

Even non-candy eaters seem to enjoy these treats, especially if they like apples. A nice change from the candied citrus that's more prevalent during the holidays, a small container makes a lovely gift.

2 pounds firm
   cooking apples
4 cups water
2 tablespoons lemon
   juice
4 cups sugar
2 cups water
1 tablespoon corn
   syrup
3 3" sticks of
   cinnamon
2 cups (approximately)
   sugar

Peel and core apples and cut into ½" thick wedges. Drop fruit into 4 cups of water mixed with the lemon juice.

In a heavy saucepan, combine 4 cups of sugar, 2 cups of water, and corn syrup. Stir over low heat until sugar is dissolved. Add cinnamon and increase the heat. Bring the mixture to a boil, without stirring and cook until a candy thermometer registers 238.° In the meantime, remove apple wedges from water with a slotted spoon and pat them dry on paper toweling. Drop apples into boiling syrup and lower heat slightly. Let wedges boil, without stirring, for approximately 15 minutes or until they look transparent and the candy thermometer goes back up to 238.° (While not actually stirring, you may need to move apples that are near the sides of the pan to the center during the cooking to be sure that all slices cook evenly.)

Preheat oven to 200.° Lower heat under apples and, using a fork or slotted spoon, remove wedges a few at a time and place on a baking sheet. Bake for approximately 1½ hours or until slices look wrinkled, but not brown. Cool slightly on rack; then dip each slice into the remaining 2 cups of sugar. Allow to cool completely before storing in a loosely covered container in a cool, dry place.

Chocolate Seafoam

Makes
3-4 dozen
pieces

Since early childhood seafoam has been one of my favorite candies. When it is chocolate seafoam, it is truly divine, but it should be saved for the confirmed sugar addict and chocoholic. For them, a small tin filled with this confection will make an infinitely satisfying gift.

2 cups firmly packed
   light brown sugar
¾ cup cold water
1 5½-ounce can
   chocolate syrup
2 egg whites
1 teaspoon vanilla
1 square baking
   chocolate, melted
½ cup coarsely
   chopped pecans or
   walnuts

Combine sugar, water and chocolate syrup in a heavy pan and cook over medium heat, stirring constantly, until the sugar dissolves and mixture boils. Continue cooking, without stirring until a candy thermometer registers 250°. Remove from heat.

Beat egg whites until very stiff. Pour hot syrup in a thin stream over beaten egg whites, beating constantly at high speed. Continue beating until mixture forms peaks when dropped from a spoon (about 10 minutes). Quickly stir in vanilla, melted chocolate and nuts. Drop by teaspoonful onto waxed paper. Allow to cool completely before packing in tightly covered tins. Store in cool, dry place.

79

Cracker Fudge

Our next door neighbors are always surprising us with thoughtful gestures— our garbage cans brought in for us on a cold and windy day... the grass beside the drive trimmed on a hot sultry summer afternoon. In addition, Mrs. Robinson, who is an excellent cook, pops in often to share goodies from her kitchen. Recently she brought over a plate of delicious creamy peanut butter fudge. You'll be as surprised as I was at her "secret" ingredient.

¼ **pound saltine crackers**
¾ **cup peanut butter**
3 **cups sugar**
1 **cup milk**

Crumble crackers into a mixing bowl and stir in peanut butter. In a small heavy saucepan, combine sugar and milk and bring to a boil. Continue to boil, stirring constantly, for five minutes. Pour over crackers and mix with electric mixer until smooth. Pour into a buttered 8"x 8" pan. Cut into 1" squares when the fudge has set. Pack into a tightly covered container, separating the layers of pieces by waxed paper and refrigerate.